CONTENTS

WHAT are PreCuT FaBriCS?

Precut fabrics are groups of coordinating fabrics that have been cut into specific sizes from yardage. They are themed by color, pattern, designer's collection, or fabric type. Typically, manufacturers make them from quilting-weight cotton fabrics. The number of pieces in each precut package varies, and often each group provides duplicates of designs.

Precut fabrics offer several advantages to sewers, quilters, and crafters. They are convenient to use and are always perfectly coordinated to offer a great assortment of print and color options that work together for any project. Precut fabrics save time as you can immediately get started on your project without the stress of selecting just the right coordinating fabrics.

Many people's least favorite activity when creating fabric projects is preparing and cutting the fabric. Precuts allow you to get started right away.

Precuts also save money since you do not have to purchase all the fabrics in a collection by the yard. In most stores, the smallest amount that staff will cut is ¼ yard (0.2 meter). If you had to purchase ¼-yard (0.2 meter) cuts of thirty different fabrics, the cost could really add up. Precuts also reduce waste as they often provide the exact sizes required for projects, with a minimal amount of trimming.

Fat Quarters

Most quilting-weight cotton fabrics are about 44" (111.8 cm) wide. A yard of fabric will measure 36" X 44" (91.4 X 111.8 cm). A quarter yard will measure 9" X 44" (22.9 X 111.8 cm), which is a long skinny size that is not always very useful. A fat quarter is also a quarter yard of fabric, but it is cut in a different way. To make a fat quarter, the fabric is first cut into a ½-yard (0.5 m) piece, measuring 18" X 44" (45.7 X 111.8 cm). Then it is cut again along the centerfold to make two fat quarters, each 18" X 22" (45.7 X 55.9 cm).

Stores sell fat quarters individually as well as in coordinating bundles wrapped together for a pretty presentation.

Using fat quarters versus quarter-yard cuts of fabric offers several advantages. Fat quarters are good for projects that require larger pieces of fabric; e.g., pillows, placemats and napkins. And fat quarters of larger-scale designs will include more of the entire printed pattern.

Fat eighths

Fat eighths are half the size of fat quarters. They are cut to measure approximately 11" X 18" (27.9 X 45.7 cm) or 9" X 22" (22.9 X 55.9 cm). They are the same amount of fabric as an eighth of a yard that has been cut across the finished width. But like a fat quarter, they are a much more useful size. Fat eighths are also sold individually or in coordinated bundles. Fat eighths are not as commonly found in stores as fat quarters. Although I did not use this size of precuts in any of the projects in this book, you may find them useful for your own designs.

fat quarters

strips

Precut strips are narrow cuts across the full width of the fabric, usually 2½" x 44" (6.4 x 111.8 cm). Strips are generally sold in groups of 20, 30, or 40 pieces. Sometimes the collections will include duplicates of the fabric prints. Different manufacturers have different names for their precut strip collections. You will hear them referred to as designer rolls or jelly rolls or other clever names. Each roll should have a tag giving information about the fabrics, including the number of duplicates and the number of strips that the bundle includes.

Precut strips give you the most variety of colors and prints in a collection, and you can piece them together in many interesting ways.

squares

Precut fabric squares are typically 5" x 5" (12.7 x 12.7 cm) or 6" x 6" (15.2 x 15.2 cm). Manufacturers refer to the coordinating bundles as charm packs or charms. They get their name from traditionally made charm quilts that had no two fabrics with the same pattern. Like precut strips, manufacturers sell charm squares in packs of 20, 30, or 40 coordinating fabric squares. Check the label for the specifics.

Larger 10" x 10" (25.4 x 25.4 cm) squares are also available in precut bundles. Different manufacturers call them different names, and you will hear them referred to as layer cakes, stackers, or other clever names.

strips

squares

WORKING WITH PRECUT FABRICS

PREPARATION

Precut fabrics are ready to use in your projects. Check the label for any care instructions. Generally speaking, I do not prewash precut fabrics. Since all of the fabrics are coming from the same collection and are printed on the same type of base fabric, any shrinkage will be equal for all the fabrics when you wash them. If you are concerned about shrinkage or colors running when washed, you can hand wash the precuts, taking care not to over-handle them. Although the cut edges of some precuts may be pinked, they will begin to unravel when agitated. Do not wash precut fabrics in the washing machine and do not put them in the dryer.

To wash fat quarters, strips, and squares by hand, separate the pieces by similar colors. Fill a large sink with cold water. Add a mild detergent and swish the water around to get the soap evenly distributed. Place the precuts in the water and very gently swirl them until they are all wet. Let the fabrics soak for 15–20 minutes. Drain the soapy water and rinse the fabrics completely under cool running water. Make sure all the soap residue is out of the fabrics. Squeeze excess water out of fabrics with a thirsty towel and lay the pieces flat to air dry a bit. Press the pieces while still damp and lightly spray with sizing to restore crispness, if desired.

Once you have completed your project and have properly finished or hidden the seam allowances, you can wash and dry the fabrics as the manufacturer instructs.

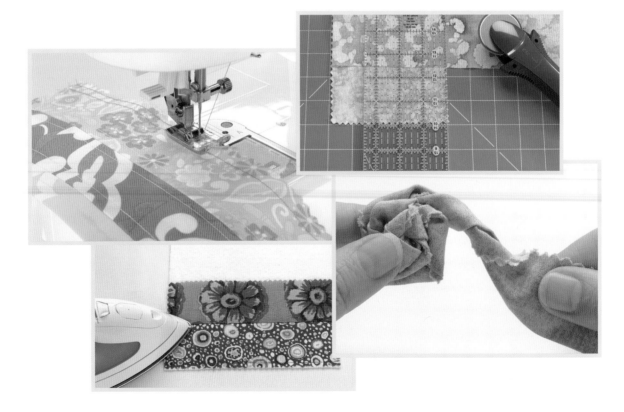

sewing with precut fabrics

Once you unroll a package of precut strips, unfold a bundle of fat quarters, or open a package of charm squares, the magic starts to happen. Look through the different fabric designs. You may want to pull out your favorites or any that you feel are accent prints. You can separate lights and darks to help you create a project that showcases the differences in the various coordinating patterns.

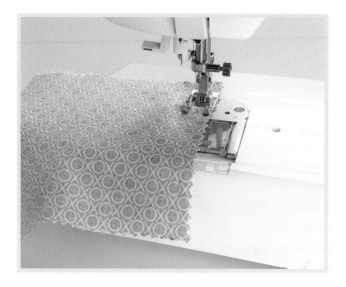

Stitching the pieces together is simple. Put the selected precuts right sides together and sew them with straight machine stitches. For most of the projects in this book, I have pieced the precuts together with a seam allowance of ¼" (6 mm) or ½" (1.3 cm). If the edges of the pieces are pinked with a zigzag edge, place the outermost tips of the zigzags along the desired marking on your sewing-machine's guides. To assure that pieces will line up and be the correct size, make sure to be consistent in sewing the seams together so the seam allowances are the same width throughout the project.

I usually do not find it necessary to pin before I stitch. If I have to adjust the edges of the precuts that I am sewing together, I stop stitching with the needle in the down position, align the edges of the precuts, and then continue stitching the seam. When sewing two patched rows together, however, I do use pins to match seams so they will align when sewn. It is a good idea to add pins to the seam allowances so they lie flat when sewn.

IRONING AND FINISHING SEAMS

One of the most important things to remember when working with precut fabrics is ironing seams flat before progressing to the next step in your project's construction. Since the vast majority of precut fabrics are 100% cotton, use a hot iron with steam.

You can either press seams to one side or press them open. Press from both the front and back of the fabric and make sure that the pressed seams are completely flat in each step.

If the seams in the project are hidden or if you will not launder the project, it is not necessary to finish the seams. Some precut strips and charm squares have pinked edges that will help to keep the fabric from fraying. Other precuts do not have this zigzag edge and if you are using them for projects that you will launder, such as aprons or skirts, it is a good idea to finish the seams. You can trim the raw edges of the precuts with pinking shears or can finish them with topstitching.

TOPSTITCHED SEAMS

Topstitching is straight machine stitching, typically sewn from the right side of the fabric. Not only does the topstitching hold the seams flat, but also it keeps the raw edges from unraveling when agitated in the washer and dryer. When you press the seams to one side, topstitch them with one row of stitching through the seam allowance, close to the seam. When you press the seams open, topstitch them on each side, close to each side of the seam line. If the seam allowances are $\frac{1}{4}$" (6 mm) wide, topstitch them $\frac{1}{8}$" (3 mm) from the seam line. If the seam allowances are $\frac{1}{2}$" (1.3 cm) wide, topstitch them $\frac{1}{4}$" (6 mm) from the seam line.

French Seams

Sometimes you do not want the raw edges of a seam allowance to be exposed, especially if the project gets lots of wear or might have to stand up to repeated laundering or if the wrong side of the fabric may show, such as with a curtain panel. For a neat finish, it is best to use a French seam. A French seam looks like a plain seam from the right side and a narrow tuck on the wrong side.

To sew a French seam:

1 Place the fabric wrong sides together.

2 Stitch ⅛" (3 mm) from the raw edges.

3 Press the seam allowance to one side.

4 Fold and press the fabric right sides together, keeping the stitching line at the center of the fold.

5 Stitch ¼" (6 mm) away from the first line of stitching. The raw edges will be encased inside the tuck. Check to make sure you have no raveled threads that are showing.

6 Press the seam to one side.

French seams are difficult to sew in curved areas, but they are perfect for finishing the many straight seams you encounter when working with precut fabrics.

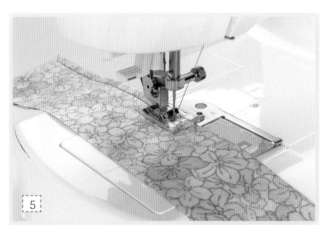

reversible
TOTE AND
CLUTCH

Many rolls of precut strips include a combination of light and dark fabrics. By separating them out into two groups, you can make a reversible tote bag—one side light colors and the other side dark colors. You can use coordinating ribbons for the handles and the pocket trim. To corral all the little things you carry that might get lost inside the large tote bag, make a small zippered clutch with the leftover bits of strips.

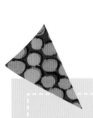

PRECUT FABRICS

- twenty 2½" (6.4 cm) strips (ten light colors and ten dark colors)
- twelve 6" (15.2 cm) squares (six light colors and six dark colors) for pockets
- one fat quarter for the clutch's lining

OTHER SUPPLIES AND TOOLS

- 2⅛ yd (1.9 meters) of 1½" (3.8 cm) coordinating ribbon, light color
- 2⅛ yd (1.9 meters) of 1½" (3.8 cm) coordinating ribbon, dark color

- 20" × 36" (50.8 × 91.4 cm) rectangle of Roc-Lon® Multi-Purpose Cloth or heavyweight nonfusible interfacing
- 20" × 36" (50.8 × 91.4 cm) rectangle of thin cotton batting
- ½" (1.3 cm) strips of fusible web
- two 6½" × 10½" (16.5 × 26.7 cm) rectangles of fusible fleece
- 12" (30.5 cm) or longer zipper for clutch
- ¾" (1.9 cm) D-ring and swivel clasp
- coordinating sewing thread
- sewing machine and iron
- usual sewing supplies

PUTTING IT TOGETHER
reversible tote

Use ½" (1.3 cm) seam allowances throughout construction of tote, unless instructed otherwise.

1 Cut 36" (91.4 cm) lengths of the 20 strips and separate them into two piles—light colors and dark colors.

2 Following the instructions for stitch–and–flip quilting (page 30), sew the dark-colored strips to the Multi-Purpose Cloth or heavyweight interfacing. Sew the light-colored strips to the cotton batting. Trim the rectangles to the same size and check that all sides are straight. The shorter sides of the rectangles will be the top edges of the tote. Fold the rectangles in half and mark the center line on the wrong side with a pencil or fabric marking pen. This area will be the bottom of the tote.

3 To make the pockets, sew the six dark-colored squares together in two rows of three squares each. In the same way, sew the six light-colored squares together.

4 Fold the pockets in half and decide which side will be the front of each; unfold. Position a dark ribbon onto the front of the dark pocket and light ribbon onto the light pocket, centering the ribbons over the horizontal seams. Use strips of fusible web to hold the ribbons in place. Sew the ribbons to the pockets.

5 Fold each pocket in half, right sides together. Starting at the fold line, sew along the sides, leaving an opening for turning.

6 Clip the corners and turn the pockets right side out. Iron the pockets, making sure to press under the seam allowances at the openings.

7 Center the light pocket onto the light side of the tote bag with the top of the pocket 4" (10.2 cm) from the raw edge. Stitch the pocket to the tote bag, close to the sides and bottom

edges. Do the same with the dark pocket on the dark side of the tote.

8 Fold the light side of the tote bag, right sides together; sew the side seams. Press the seams open. Repeat for the dark side.

9 To shape the bottom of the tote, align the side seams with the marked center line. Flatten the triangle formed and stitch straight across it, 1¾" (4.5 cm) from the point. Repeat for both pieces. Slip-stitch the triangles to the bottom of the bag.

10 To make the handles, cut each remaining ribbon into two equal lengths. You will have four ribbon lengths—two light and two dark.

With the wrong sides together, fuse the light ribbons to the dark ribbons. Sew close to the long edges with your machine's straight, zigzag, or blanket stitches.

11 Position the light side of the handles against the light sides of the tote. Align the raw edges of the handles with the top edge of the tote. Place the outer edge of the handles 4" (10.2 cm) in from each side seam. Baste the edges to hold them.

12 Place the right side of the light side of the tote against the right side of the dark side. The sides with the pockets should be against the sides without the pockets. Align the raw edges, matching the side seams. Stitch the top edges together, leaving an opening for turning.

13 Turn the tote right side out through the opening. Push the light side of the bag into the dark side. Iron the top edge of the tote, making sure to press back the seam allowances of the opening. Slip-stitch the opening

closed. Hand baste close to the top edge to hold the layers together. Using a heavy machine needle, top stitch ¼" (6 mm) from the finished edge. Remove the basting stitches.

CLUTCH BaG

1   Cut two 6½" × 10½" (16.5 × 26.7 cm) rectangles from the fat quarter for the bag lining. Following manufacturer's instructions, iron the fusible-fleece rectangles to the back of the fabric rectangles.

2   From leftover strips used for tote bag, cut ten 6½" (16.5 cm) strips. If you like, you can divide them in half and use the light colors for one side of the clutch and dark colors for the other side. Following the instructions for stitch-and-flip quilting (page 30), sew five strips to the fleece side of each rectangle. Trim the rectangles to the same size, even with the edge of the fabric strips.

3   Cut two 1½" (3.8 cm) lengths of strips to cover the ends of the zipper. Fold each in half lengthwise, wrong sides together, and press them. Press the raw edges to meet at the center crease. Refold and press again.

4   Stitch across the zipper teeth near the zipper stop at the bottom of the zipper. Cut the zipper stop off. Unzip the zipper several inches. Trim the zipper 1" (2.5 cm) shorter than the top measurement of the bag sections. Make sure not to cut off the zipper pull.

5   Insert the ends of the zipper into the folded strips and stitch close to the fold. Trim excess fabric even with the edge of the zipper.

6   With the right sides together, center the zipper on the top of one bag section. The zipper pull faces the right side of the pieced rectangle

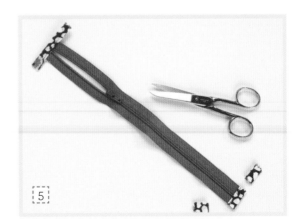

and the edge of the zipper aligns with the edge of the rectangle. Use a zipper foot and stitch the zipper to the top of the bag with a

¼" (6 mm) seam allowance. Finish the seam with a zigzag stitch to prevent the raw edges of the fabric from raveling.

7. Fold the bag section away from the zipper and pin. Topstitch close to the fold to hold the zipper tape in place.

8. Repeat Steps 6 and 7 to attach the second bag section to the other side of the zipper.

9. To make the handle and loop for the D-ring, cut a 16" (40.6 cm) strip of fabric. If necessary, sew together two or three leftover pieces to make a long-enough strip. Fold the strip in half lengthwise, with the wrong sides together, and press it. Press raw edges to meet at the center crease. Refold and press again. Stitch close to both sides.

10. Cut a 2½" (6.4 cm) length of the finished strip and insert it into the D-ring. Line up the raw edges and stitch close to form the loop. Align the raw edges of the loop with the right side of one edge of the bag, about ½" (1.3 cm) down from the zipper. Stitch a scant ¼" (6 mm) to hold.

11. Unzip the zipper halfway. Fold the bag right sides together. Sew a ¼" (6 mm) seam along the sides and the bottom of the bag. Make sure the tab and the previous stitching lines are caught in the side seams. Zigzag the edges of the seam allowance together to prevent raveling.

12. If you would like to shape the bottom of the clutch, align the side seams with the bottom seam. Flatten the triangles formed at each side and stitch straight across them, 1" (2.5 cm) from the point.

13. Turn the clutch right side out. To make the handle, slide the swivel clasp onto the remainder of the strip sewn in Step 9. Fold under one raw end ¼" (6 mm). Slip the opposite end underneath and stitch across all layers to hold them. Clip the handle onto the D-ring.

HOBO BaG

You'll need five coordinating fat-quarter prints to make this soft hobo-style bag. You use two fat quarters for the outside and two for the lining. You use the fifth one to make the handles and an inside divided pocket.

YOU WILL NEED

PRECUT FABRICS

- five fat quarters

OTHER SUPPLIES AND TOOLS

- 9" (22.9 cm) round dinner or paper plate
- polyester fiberfill
- long pencil or dowel
- 14" (35.6 cm) of ¾" (1.9 cm) elastic
- large safety pin
- coordinating sewing thread
- sewing machine and iron
- usual sewing supplies

PUTTING IT TOGETHER

Use ½" (1.3 cm) seam allowances throughout the construction of the bag.

1   Iron all fat quarters and set one aside for the handle and inside pocket. Place the fat quarters for the lining right sides together. On top of the lining pieces, place the outside fat quarters right sides together. With a rotary cutter and ruler, trim the four fat quarters to the same exact size. Make sure all the sides are straight and parallel. Trim away the selvage edges.

2   From the fifth fat quarter, cut two 3" × 22" (7.6 × 55.9 cm) rectangles for the handles. Set aside. For the pocket, fold the remainder of the fat quarter in half lengthwise, with the right sides together, and stitch along the long edge, forming a tube. Turn the tube right side out and press it, keeping the seam line along the edge.

(continued)

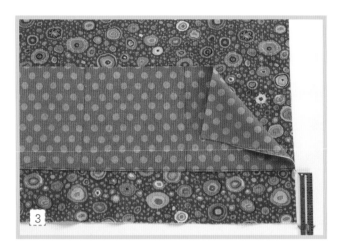

3 Place the pocket onto one of the lining fat quarters, 2½" (6.4 cm) from one long side. This side will be the bottom of the bag lining. Sew close to the lower edge. Sew four vertical parallel lines to divide the pocket into sections. You do not need to stitch the sides of the pocket as you will catch them in the side seams of the bag.

4 To form the curved lower edges of the bag, place the right sides of the lining pieces together. Position the dinner plate in the corner so that the edges touch the sides and bottom of the lining pieces. Trace the curved edge onto each bottom corner and trim away the excess fabric. Do the same with the outside pieces.

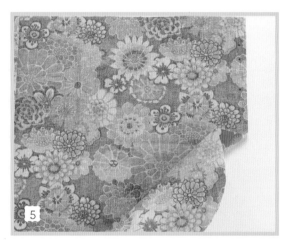

5 On both lining and outside pieces, mark three points on each side 2" (5 cm), 3" (7.6 cm) and 5" (12.7 cm) from the top straight edge.

6 With the outside pieces right sides together, sew around the sides and bottom of the bag from one 5" (12.7 cm) mark to the other 5" (12.7 cm) mark. Clip the seam allowances at the curves so that they will lie flat when you turn the bag right side out. Do the same with the lining pieces, leaving a 6" (15.2 cm) opening at the bottom for turning.

7 Turn the outside of the bag right side out. Place the lining over the outside, right sides together. Pin the top edges of the lining to the outside on each side of the bag. Pin the sides together from the 5" (12.7 cm) marks up to the top. Sew the lining to the bag at the upper sides and top. Leave an opening in the stitching between the 2" (5 cm) and 3" (7.6 cm) marks. This creates the casing at the top of the bag. Trim excess fabric from corners and turn the bag right side out through the lining opening. Slip-stitch the opening closed and push the lining into the bag.

8 To form the casing, sew two lines of stitches 1½" (3.8 cm) and 2½" (6.4 cm) from the top finished edge of both sides of the bag.

9 Fold each handle piece in half lengthwise, with right sides together. Stitch along the long edge, leaving the ends open. Turn the handles right side out. Stuff each handle with fiberfill, leaving the ends free of fiberfill. Use a long pencil or dowel to push the fiberfill firmly into the handles.

10 Sew across the ends of the handles. Cut the elastic into two 7" (17.8 cm) lengths. Overlap ½" (1.3 cm) of one end of each elastic length over one end of each handle and stitch it securely.

11 Attach a large safety pin to the ends of the elastic and thread each handle through each casing.

12 Overlap the remaining elastic and handle ends and stitch. Pull the elastic into the casing to cover the stitched ends. Sew the ends of both casings ¼" (6 mm) from the edges to hold the handles in place.

sleepover
Duffle Bag

Sleepovers are fun, whether at a friend's house or on a trip to Grandma's. Why not make a special duffle bag for the occasion? Using a die or electric fabric cutter allows you to use both positive and negative shapes for the appliquéd hearts that decorate the bag. Coordinating fat quarters and strips mixed together gives a different appearance to each side of the bag.

YOU WILL NEED

PRECUT FABRICS

- six fat quarters
- twelve 6" (15.2 cm) charm squares
- six 2½" (6.4 cm) strips

OTHER SUPPLIES AND TOOLS

- die-cutting machine cutter with heart shape
- four 6" (15.2 cm) squares fusible web
- coordinating sewing thread
- large safety pin
- sewing machine and iron
- usual sewing supplies

PUTTING IT TOGETHER

Use ½" (1.3 cm) seam allowances throughout construction of the bag and pillow case.

DUFFLE BAG

1 Select four charm squares for the contrast heart appliqués. Iron fusible web to the back of each.

2 Following the manufacturer's instructions, cut a 3½" (8.9 cm) heart from the center of each square. You will use both the cut-out heart and the remaining outside fabric as appliqués.

3 Following the appliqué instructions (page 32), fuse and sew the hearts and the squares with the cut-out hearts onto the centers of the remaining eight squares.

4 To make the front and back of the bag, sew four squares together, alternating colors. Press the seams open and topstitch them.

5 Sew a strip to the top and the bottom of the sewn squares. Trim excess fabric from ends. Press the seams open and topstitch them.

6 For the bottom of the front and back of the bag, select two fat quarters and cut a rectangle 5" × 21" (12.7 × 53.3 cm) from each. Save the remainder of the fat quarters for the bottom of the bag lining. Sew the rectangles to the bottom strips of both the front and back of the bag. Press the seams open and topstitch them.

7 Sew the long side of a fat quarter to the top strips of the front and back of the bag. Trim excess fabric straight, if necessary. Press the seams open and topstitch them.

8 To make the lining for each side of the bag, sew the long side of a fat quarter to the remainder of the fat quarter cut in Step 6. Press the seams open.

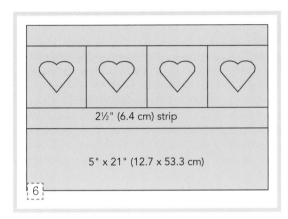

2½" (6.4 cm) strip

5" x 21" (12.7 x 53.3 cm)

6

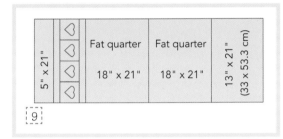

5" x 21"

Fat quarter
18" x 21"

Fat quarter
18" x 21"

13" x 21"
(33 x 53.3 cm)

9

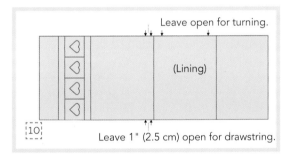

Leave open for turning.

(Lining)

10

Leave 1" (2.5 cm) open for drawstring.

14

9 Sew the linings to the top of each side of the bag. Press the seams open. Trim excess fabric straight, if necessary, to create one long rectangle.

10 Place the front and back of bag right sides together and pin them. Stitch around the bag, leaving a large opening in the lining for turning and leaving two small openings, one on each side at the top of the bag, for the drawstring casing. The casing openings should be

1" (2.5 cm) long and begin ½" (1.3 cm) from the top seam that joins the bag and lining.

11 Clip excess fabric from the corners; turn the bag and lining right side out. Press seam allowances under at the lining opening and slip-stitch the opening closed.

12 Push the bag lining into the bag. Press the seam between the bag and lining at the top edge. Topstitch ¼" (6 mm) from the edge.

13 To form the drawstring casing, stitch again 1½" (3.8 cm) from the top edge, making sure the inside seam allowances are open and flat.

14 To make the drawstrings, iron the remaining two strips in half. Press the cut edges to the center folded edge of each strip. Fold the strip in half and press it.

15 Sew close to the long side of each folded strip.

16 Attach the safety pin to the end of one drawstring and thread it through the casing, beginning and ending at one side. Overlap the raw edges of the drawstring and stitch them. Pull the drawstring through the casing so that you hide the overlap.

17 Starting from the opposite side, thread the second drawstring through the casing. Overlap the ends, stitch and pull the drawstring through the casing so the ends do not show.

18 Close the bag by pulling on both drawstrings to tightly gather up the bag opening.

BarGELLO
YOGA MaT BaG

Carry your yoga mat to class in style with this easy-to-carry shoulder bag. You construct the bag with a Bargello patchwork technique that a traditional needlework stitch inspired. The light to dark shades of color in a roll of precut strips are perfect for creating the zigzag pattern.

YOU WILL NEED

PRECUT FABRICS

- eighteen 2½" (6.4 cm) strips
- two fat quarters for the lining

OTHER SUPPLIES AND TOOLS

- 20" x 35" (50.8 x 88.9 cm) rectangle of fleece or thin batting
- two 35" (88.9 cm) lengths of 1½" (3.8 cm) ribbon to coordinate with fabrics
- ¼" (6 mm) fusible-web tape
- coordinating sewing thread
- sewing machine and iron
- usual sewing supplies

PUTTING IT TOGETHER

Use a ½" (1.3 cm) seam allowance unless instructed otherwise.

1 Cut 27" (68.6 cm) lengths from 17 of the fabric strips. Arrange the lengths in an interesting pattern of light and dark colors.

2 With a ¼" (6 mm) seam allowance, sew the strips together along the long edges to create one large pieced rectangle. Press the seam allowances in one direction toward the bottom strip.

3 Press the seam allowances in one direction toward the bottom strip.

4 Sew the remaining two long edges together, creating a cylinder of fabric with the seams on the outside. Press the remaining seam allowance in the same direction as the other seams.

5 Flatten the cylinder and trim the edge if necessary to straighten it. The cut edge should be perpendicular to the fold of the cylinder to assure that the rows of patches will be straight. Use your ruler and rotary cutter to cut rows across the cylinder. Cut one 2½" (6.4 cm)-wide strip (A), seven 2" (5 cm)-wide strips (B), two 1¾" (4.5 cm)-wide strips (C), and two 2¼" (5.7 cm)-wide strips (D).

6 Starting with an A strip, decide what fabric print you would like to have at the bottom square of the first patchwork row. Use a seam ripper to undo the seam at that point and make a long strip.

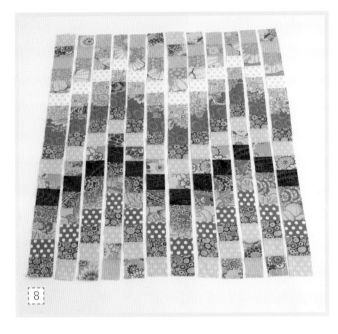

7   Place the first strip on your work table. Holding a B strip, locate the seam that is one row lower than the one you undid on the first strip and remove the stitches to make a long strip. This change will advance the fabric patterns up one row. Place it on your work surface next to the A strip.

8   Arrange the twelve strips cut from the cylinder in the following pattern: A, B, B, C, B, B, D, B, B, C, B, D. Cut the strips at the seams where the cut will allow the fabric patterns to advance up through strip C and then down to strip D two times.

9   Place the first strip A along the long edge of the fleece rectangle and stitch ¼" (6 mm) from the edge. Using the stitch-and-flip quilting technique (page 30), sew the remaining 11 strips to the fleece, pressing well after you sew each strip.

10 Trim excess fleece from the rectangle and make sure the edges are straight and perpendicular to each other.

(continued)

[11]

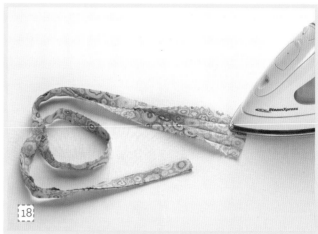

[18]

11   To make the handle, place the two ribbon lengths right sides together and sew the short edges together. Turn the ribbons right side out and press the seams. Apply strips of fusible-web tape to the edges of one of the ribbons. Following the manufacturer's instructions, fuse the two ribbons wrong sides together. Sew machine blanket or zigzag stitches along both long edges.

12   Center and pin the handle ends over the middle seam of the patchwork, 7½" (19 cm) from the bottom and 8½" (216 mm) from the top. Stitch the ends in place.

13   For the lining, sew the two fat quarters together along the long edge. Press the seam open. Trim the rectangle the same size as the patchwork rectangle.

14   With the right sides together, fold the patchwork rectangle in half lengthwise. Stitch along the bottom and side edges. Press the side seam open and turn the tube inside out.

15   Fold the lining in half lengthwise, with the right sides together. Stitch along the bottom and side edges, leaving an opening in the side seam for turning. Press the seam open.

16   Place the right side of lining against the right side of the bag. Stitch them together along the top edge.

17   Turn the bag right side out through the lining opening. Slip-stitch the opening closed. Push the lining into the bag. Iron the top edge of the bag and topstitch ¼" (6 mm) from the edge.

18   For the ties, cut a 33" (83.8 cm) length of fabric from the remaining strip. Fold up the seam allowances and press the raw edges on the short ends. Fold and press the strip in half. Fold and press the raw edges along the long edges to the center crease. Fold the strip in half and press it.

19 Stitch the piece close to all sides of the ties. Fold the tie in half, marking the center with a pin. Place the center over the side seam of the bag, 3" (7.6 cm) from the top edge. Stitch across the tie to hold it.

Make It Yours

- Instead of ribbon, you can make the handle for the bag from two precut strips sewn together. Before stitching, apply fusible interfacing to the wrong side of both strips to make the handle sturdy.

- Sew together leftover bits of strips to make a trim to decorate a coordinating towel or make a small zippered bag.

- Bargello patchwork makes a beautiful wall hanging or quilt. Decide the height of the piece you want to make and divide by 2 to determine the number of strips you will need. Sew the strips together into a cylinder and cut the strips across as described above. The strips can be all the same size or can vary in width. Undo the strips so that the colors and prints of the fabric will advance up and down across the piece. Sew the strips together. Quilt and bind the piece or stretch the pieced fabric over a stretcher frame to create a wall hanging.

- Bargello patchwork is a great way to use up random leftover, precut strips from other projects.

STITCH AND FLIP QUILTING

This quilt-as-you-go technique is great to use with precut fabric strips and squares. It allows you to sew pieces together and quilt them to a batting or background fabric at the same time.

Begin by selecting the background onto which you want to quilt the pieces. In most of the projects in this book, I have quilted the precuts onto thin fleece or batting or fusible fleece that I have ironed onto a background fabric.

1 With the right side up, place the first precut piece of fabric along the outer edge of the batting or backing fabric and stitch close to the outer edge.

2 Place the second piece on top of the first, right sides together. Stitch them together ¼" (6 mm) from the raw edge. The stitches will also secure the pieces to the batting or backing fabric.

3 Flip the second piece back so that it is right side up. Press it flat.

4 Continue to sew on pieces one at a time, flipping and ironing each piece as you sew it.

5 From time to time, use a clear ruler to make sure that the stitched rows are parallel to the beginning edge. If necessary, make small adjustments to the stitching lines to keep them even and straight. Small adjustments will not be noticeable in the finished project, but it is important to continue to check the measurements before the rows become too much out of alignment.

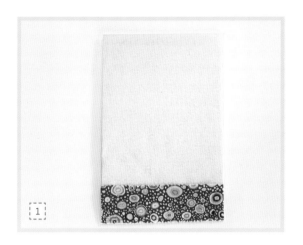

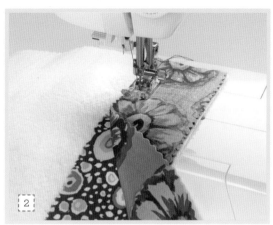

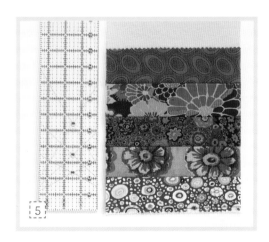

APPLIQUÉ

Appliqué means to "place upon." Fabric appliqués are cut-out decorations attached to a background fabric. Traditionally, you cut out shapes, turn back the raw edges, and handstitch the designs to the background. Now with the use of paper-backed fusible web, you can quickly fuse the appliqués in place with an iron and then machine- or handstitch them to decoratively finish the edges.

Following the manufacturer's instructions, iron fusible web to the back of a precut square or left-over bit of any precut piece. When it's cool, draw or trace a design onto the paper backing and cut it out. Note that if the design is one-way, such as an alphabet letter, you need to draw the reverse image of the design so that the right side of the fabric will be face up to appliqué in place.

The easiest way to make an appliqué design is to use one of the many shapes available on a manual or electronic fabric die-cutting machine. This technique requires no drawing, and the cutting is quick and accurate.

Remove the paper from the back of the appliqué and iron the shape to your project. If you will launder the project or it will be subject to wear, finish the edges with hand or machine stitches, such as straight, blanket, or satin stitch.

With a little planning, you can efficiently use every scrap of a precut square. The advantage of using a cutting machine is that you do not have to cut into the fabric to cut out the shape. The blade of the cutter just cuts the line around the design, leaving you with the design and the reverse image cut from the fabric. You can use both pieces in a project. To do so, make sure to center the appliqué design in the square on the cutting machine. You can appliqué both the positive and negative image to your project.